Intense feeling, empathy, rage, compassion swerves language, torques the page. History and data inflict. Intelligence ⬚⬚⬚⬚⬚⬚⬚⬚⬚ ce. It must be witnessed, expressed. The love is expression. Witness is form.

*Mei-m⬚⬚⬚⬚⬚⬚⬚⬚⬚pen*

Read Cody's investigations, these beyond-poems, the Treaty of Guadalupe Hidalgo of 1848, Mexican Indian lands, the untold occupations of America—as if you are hanging on that open-air killing tree. Notice the vortex of existence, yours, ours, the trapezoids of punishments, the dotted lines and splattered shapes of skin-text and the searing howls cut down the middle of the word bodies, usurpation, rape and theft bursting across the emptiness pages, terminations and exiles pinned on the Race Grid. Open these scrolls and peer at half-humanity América cutting you down, dangling—there is no wall after all, just a mirror of executions, "reach for the hand of a friend" "in a dream," you are the "savage captured," the "KickingSingingKickingSinging chant," you are the segmented ink-jitters on Cody's pages, you are the "atomic" Brown radiating yourself out of the 1850's into this present of border mania. Read Cody's script, like no other—a photo-zoom of tragic roots and revelations, cartographies of "power and control," and the transcendence of innocent bodies, somehow—American soul. Cody presents what has not been revealed, what must be said. This one-of-a-kind-book settles all cases against all border-crossers. It is possible: a brave, bold syntax, an unseen intelligence of ourselves, a new America. Bravo for these compassionate and brutal time-spaces, this brisling land voice—an exemplar of a bursting literature. Everything starts over now.

*Juan Felipe Herrera*

Because the document is always part of poetry in the general sense Shelley wrote about. Because the concept never did exceed politics or position. Because everything must change. Because the unaccountable, the disavowed, the apocryphal are the only metadata you'll find in our nudes. Because whiteness is an extractive enterprise. Because patriarchy would look us in the face and think we'll keep its secrets. Because with this history we're not trying to accept the choice between having been colonizer or colonized. Because who, if we're embraced or estranged from whiteness to suit whiteness, would hear us among the racial orders? Because vigilance committees now have Facebook groups, publicly funded military-grade weapons and surveillance technologies. Because our bodies are monetized in private prisons and in political speech. Because we're not trying to confuse our faces with our masks. Because from the formal exigencies of document and concept, Anthony Cody delivers poetry back to the general sense of ritual and charm, a gnosis that takes its shape at the double edge of the words and the transmitting body. And because everything must change, the transit leads from here to the dead and back.

*Farid Matuk*

History's true story is littered with collusions, silences, and with bodies: the dark ecology Anthony Cody brilliantly prosecutes in his debut collection, *Borderland Apocrypha*. This book creates a new mechanism of critique through its forensic and conspiratorial speaker who gathers the dearth of evidence left behind by imperialism's worse offenders and parses out a thrilling and trenchant document on the U.S. West's legacy of anti-Mexican bigotry. "The inheritance of the elsewhere is a cave of collapse," writes Cody in a collection that will change the way we think about recovering histories.

*Carmen Giménez Smith*

T0069134

# borderland

## apocrypha

# borderland apocrypha

## anthony cody

© Copyright Anthony Cody, 2020. All rights reserved.

Cover art by Josué Rojas
(Front cover: "Appropriate Strategies No. 2" and back cover: "Appropriate Strategies No. 1")

Cover and interior set in Octavian MT Std and Perpetua Std

Cover and interior design by Gillian Olivia Blythe Hamel

Printed in the United States
by Books International, Dulles, Virginia
On 50# Glatfelter B19 Antique
Acid Free Archival Quality Recycled Paper

Library of Congress Cataloging-in-Publication Data

Names: Cody, Anthony, 1981- author.
Title: Borderland apocrypha / Anthony Cody.
Description: Oakland, California : Omnidawn Publishing, [2020]
Identifiers: LCCN 2019049154 | ISBN 9781632430762 (trade paperback)
Subjects: LCSH: Lynching--Mexico--Poetry. | LCGFT: Poetry.
Classification: LCC PS3603.O29548 B67 2020 | DDC 811/.6--dc23
LC record available at https://lccn.loc.gov/2019049154

Published by Omnidawn Publishing, Oakland, California
www.omnidawn.com    (510) 237-5472    (800) 792-4957
10 9 8 7 6 5 4 3 2 1
ISBN: 978-1-63243-076-2

*Escribir es buscar en el tumulto de los quemados el hueso del brazo que corresponda al hueso de la pierna. Miserabla mixture. Yo restauro, yo reconstruyo, yo ando así de rodeada de muerte.*

*To write is to rummage through a tumult of burnt bodies, for the arm bone that corresponds to the leg bone. A miserable mixture. I restore, I reconstruct, so surrounded am I by death.*

*Alejandra Pizarnik*
*translated by Yvette Siegert*
*from "Extracting the Stone of Madness"*

# Contents

{one}

# Standing in line to take a passport photo,

I am
a lot of
things        and since
I am
a lot of
things
I am
everything
he cannot
imagine[2]

asks
me                              to 2x2
                                myself

and capture
what                            I am
                                in neutral

and I
recall                          I have
                                yet to see

the chambers
of my heart                     turn
                                tusk[3]

here
because my grandpa
                        ran away
from home
to sell perfume en el Zócalo
at 9[1]

# an old white man looks at me and claims I am running

is not
Gil Scott-Heron,
saying:
*Because I always feel*
*like*
*running, not away*
*because*
*there is no such place*

is not
how you pronounce:
exile or
escapar[4]

I am afraid,

no,

I am a wall,

no,

I am a mirror[6]

how Teddy Roosevelt died coveting a white buffalo[5]

still,                    so
still[7]

Standing here because my grandpa ran away from home to sell perfume en el Zócalo at 9[1]

the static in the airwaves
remains a backbone
crackling in a shadow
the daylight cannot remember

en la caravana del hambre

fuga en la calle

agarra el sombrero

un ángulo de hombro

after        his        father
died.              followed
his    brother,    dolo-
res,  named  after  child-
birth,  &  later  murdered
by         his       grandson,
who         hung      himself
in     prison,         unable
to  await  trial,  a  vigilance
committee,            dangling

conceal the juncture / masquerade the way

[vetiver rosehips cedarwood lavender]

the way across / is not the path into

[clove chamomile bergamot]

the trench / the trench without space

[sandalwood palmrosa geranium sage]

tooth / tooth an aperture underneath

                                                              trade
                                        all the pencils
                                                              owned
                                        for a pocketknife
                                        at school (etched
                                        on the handle,
                                        a labrador growls
                                        at a pheasant)
                                                              gift
cucurrucucú                             this to your mother for
until mother                            weeks
means michoacán                                        scrape
          then cucurrucucú              scavenged
                leaving                      lead into sentences
          to cross san ysidro                          graded

[the soundless gasp impeels sky]

In line I am a lot of things and since I am a lot of things I am everything he cannot imagine[2]

appear in lists:
[5 things to Improve Your Love Life] [3 Easy Meals to Cook on The Go] [5 Signs You Really Are A Bad Person] [Treaty of Guadalupe Hidalgo] [Chavez Ravine] [Prop. 187] [SB1070] [SB4] [Operation Wetback] [...]

[HangingTree][Orange,TX][8/18/1888]

ANonchalanceOfWhiteBoys

BloodOnAWhiteShirtStains

Defiance:ArmsCrossedStaringAtCamera

you wait. feel
the soles
            flatten
you      cross. you
            cargo. you
            carry. you
            quiet. you
            come. you
            invite others.

here    not leaving here    not putting my hands up    not willing to vacate the premises    not nothing    not running    not invisible    not the quiet crinkle of a body bag not me not you not me not you not me not you not me not you not me not you not me not you I am I am I am I am I am I am I am I am I am I am I am I am I am I am:

The echo of your extinction.
The bones buried.
The month of rememberance uttered in a dead tongue.

19

# A passport photo asks me to 2x2 myself and capture what I am in neutral

should be

    mailed
    to the
    federal
    govern-
    ment

with
my birth certificate.
and i wonder
if they will return

    (con-
    sid-
    er
    the
    pow-
    er
    of
    print-
    ed
    pa-
    per)

daily
am i
brown?
am i
white?
am i ?
i am.
am i ?
i am.
am i ?
i am.
i am.
i wonder
when the tense
transitions?

a neat shape

tells you no lies

raises no questions

[pure]

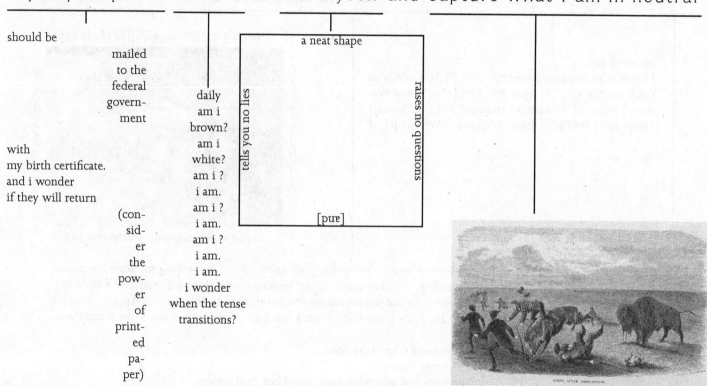

and I recall I have yet to see the chamber of my heart turn tusk[3]

a sunrise
in the shadow    or a child
birth            itself
                                    from the
                        inside of a joshua tree
                                        and
                                this does not
                        mean it is not possible

                                                    is a quiet,

            quiet,
            the outside of a pulse driving into a fire

turn dusk
turn day
turn lengua
turn lingua
turn franca
turn español
turn sombra
así
atrás
allí
acá
to here
yes
here
yes
here it is dark

An old white man is not Gil-Scott Heron saying: because I always feel like running n[o]

dies on the same day
astronauts aboard En-
deavor walk on what
is perceived the final
walk in space by NASA

and was born 97 years
to the day Carlos Esclava
was lynched for theft in
Mokelumne Hill, CA be-
fore a crowd of ~1,000

in the night          the air is what i find
is a round patch of scar at the end of [h]
and I cradle it                he says
I do not pull away     want to
and a spider appears           says it is a f[]

is now my father
was once his father
and one day a stranger
may assume
I am

way because there is no such place is not how you pronounce exile or escapar[4]

dream        when i reach for the hand of a friend       all that remains

ght arm      he does not skip a beat and places the limb in my palm

as been a long time since we touched        this is true

he laughs       pulls away and does a handstand with his good arm

era window      he crawls through      stands      waves goodbye

is not:      a choice

but:      the shape of a hand carving
itself moonlight

like exhale
like missile
like monkey
like key
like a door
that must be opened and while a clave exists
you cannot make it from your mouth

# Looks at me how Teddy Roosevelt died coveting a white buffalo[5]

as a mirror
and a mirror
has
        no voice
in the exchange.

was drawn by Martín Ramírez. Or so I have now invented. The Red Rider, frenzy-eyed and bullet fashioned, may in fact leap from a horse that will buck him off first. Teddy is gnawed in a manor of mirrors inside a forest of cartography. He is going west. He will be institutionalized, tuberculosis and schizophrenia. He will not not be president. Martín has conjured a labyrinth, he walks through, Teddy stays.

sounds like averice
or manifest destiny
or the sound a man
makes when saying
nothing and buying
the entire southwest
for $15m to make
the Americas
singular and possessive.

i find grandpa's

the things required

alien registration card

in a box of tools

is a static word    used by people
to tell others a movement or a person
is final and gone.
                    what if i write: i breathed in
the air of my grandma the moment she became atomic.
                    what if
i write: outside of what the human eye can see
the atomic is infinite.                    what if i write:
                    a border
can be built or razed, but never atomic.

Claims I am afraid, no, I am a wall, no, I am a mirror[6]

on gold
        mines
in California
      have
      dropped
since
the 1840s
      while market claims
against
      Mexicans
to go back to where they
came from
      have grown
steadily

a beetle
scuttling into

and incising

tomorrow

are you okay
I reply

your
throat
the vocal
chords
before
your
children
ask

I am

and ask to see myself          ask to see myself
      to find that I am

      nothing

          more than          light
                       telling
                       itself

I exist
yes          I exist
          yes

of digging
                for doors
      only opened from above
or elections
                that ask
      you to be afraid

is just another name for sand

I am still, so still[7]

birthed
& crawling & chueco
        scarred & bald

clean un-
clean born un-
                    born
                    & blooming

                fallow
inside concrete
cracks & fields
learning the kidneys, too,
            have fashioned
        an eschaton of stars
        to impugn possession.

{two}

Prelude to a Mexican Lynching, February 2, 1848, Guadalupe Hidalgo; or The Treaty of Peace, Friendship, Limits, and Settlement

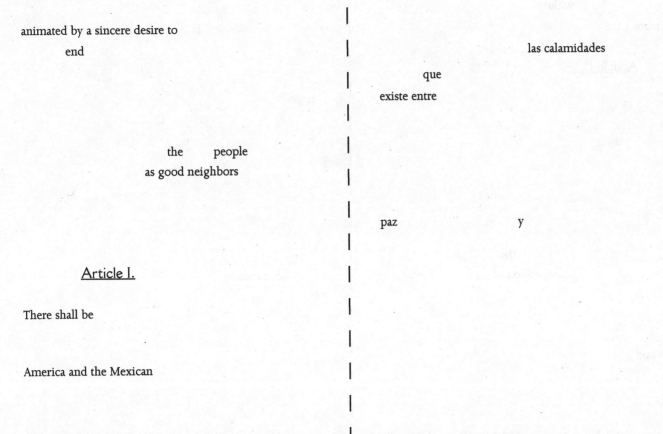

animated by a sincere desire to
end

las calamidades

que
existe entre

the        people
as good neighbors

paz                    y

Article I.

There shall be

America and the Mexican

ciudades

without                    sin

place                                              personas

Article II.                     Luego

enter

the
suspension of                              ocupado

the said

32

## Article III.

Immediately

tierra

blockading

any Mexican

se consume

para

tiempo

not yet fallen

y

los derechos

from

the cost of collection

The evacuation
of the Mexican

shall be

en el presente

soon

antes si fuere posible.

## Article IV.

all castles, forts, territories, places, and possessions
    have been taken

las fuerzas de
    la presente guerra,

van a fijarse

with                       the
    apparatus of

        the said

      securing

destruction

35

of the Mexican

rendering it

convenient

If

the Mexican

friendly

healthy and otherwise suitable

should now be held as captive
within                    the United States


dentro de la linea

que toca

la devolución
de la república

hasta

no se hayan

alguna

libertad

36

<u>Article V.</u>

el Norte

the mouth

  should have

    the deepest channel

    until it empties

The      limits

La línea

corta

el primero brazo    y si no está

cortado

el Río

separa

los que  marcan

37

                    the

                    map

preclude all

                                                                        sobre la tierra


                                        to designate
    the boundary line with             authoratative
maps
                the mouth


        journals              all          deemed
                                           necessary.


                boundary line              shall be
religious

                                                                                y ninguna

                                                                                    libre

38

## Article VI.

The      citizens of the United States shall     have
a free and uninterrupted passage

                 by land, without the express consent of
the Mexican

      it should be ascertained to be practicable and
advantageous                         que                el

                                      fin

## Article VII.

el Norte lying

 

 

any work       may

 

 

be levied upon       persons

landing upon       the      shores

Como

 

se dividen

la parte que queda

 

 

sin

los       que quedan

## Article VIII.

Mexicans                                          remain

                                     defined by

where they now reside,

                                   being subjected

         or                        whatever

Those who            remain

        shall be under the obligation to

      declare their              character

every           Mexican not established

    shall be

       property

## Article IX.

Mexicans

no conserven el carácter de ciudadanos

conform

in the free exercise of                    restriction

## Article X.

[Stricken    ]

## Article XI.

Consider

the limits

of the                            savage

serían

el                                  gobierno

contra

captured

property            cosas                              robado

43

Y                                          personas

                    through the faithful

    exercise of    influence and power, to

                              deliver

                                    y el              Mexicano pagara los gastos

                                          queda

    lost sight                      for the removal
    of the Indians from any portion of the    territories

                                                                    en necesidad

44

<u>Article XII.</u>

consider the     acquired

the boundaries     the       defined     the

article    the present     the government

después                 de la

plata

corren

as it

falls

## Article XIII.

liquidate

the Mexican

for the future,

## Article XIV.

The                    discharge                              of

the Mexican

shall be          perpetual

hasta aquí
se venzan

decididas    contra el gobierno

que habla
y cualquiera que pueda ser

Article XV.

        exonerating

                                            de toda responsibilidad

                                                    siempre                          toman

su cargo

                                        para fijar el

                                                fallo                        y

claimants, any books, records, or documents

the United States                                      cada demanda,

                               sin

                                  la verdad

## Article XVI.

reserves to itself

the entire right to fortify whatever

su seguridad

## Article XVII.

conclude

the United States of America

reserves to itself the right, at any time

to terminate                                    the other

## Article XVIII.

of the

troops

shall be

exempt from duties and charges of any kind

empeña

la sombra

it shall be the duty of all
nounce        the Mexican

to de-

como

castigado

## Article XIX.

With respect

　　　　　Mexico

　　　　　　　　　　　　　　　　　　　　　　　han estado ocupados

1.

　　　　　　　　　　　　　　　　　　　　　　　　　　　　Mexicanas

　　　　　　　　　　　shall be prohibited

2. The　　　　　perfect

　　　　　　　　　　　　　　　　　　　que lleguen　　　　　　　　　después

　　　　　Mexican　　　　　being

　　　　subject to

　　　　　　　following

3. All

　　　　　　　　　　　　　　　　　quedarán exentos de todo derecho,

shall    be    subject    to       sale

4. All

          shall have been removed

     from every kind of               title or

nation

5.               merchandise, effects, property

       shall be removed         by the

forces of the United States

                                      las leyes

                                         a

6.                                    Los dueños

or              whatever

With respect                 any Mexican

shall

pay                                                     del gobierno

## Article XX.
for the interests of commerce

hasta           la devolución

the Mexican

shall be admitted    entry

## Article XXI.

disagreement should        arise

la hostilidad

crea

deemed     altogether incompatible

Article XXII.

God forbid!

as

absolute obvervance shall be impossible

Upon the entrance of the armies                    into the territories
of the other, women and children, ecclesiastics, scholars of every
faculty, cultivators of the earth, merchants, artisans, manufac-
turers, and fisherman, unarmed adn inhabiting unfortified towns,
villages, or places, and in general all persons whose occupations
are for the common subsistence and benefit of mankind shall be

el mundo,    observa

la naturaleza

1.

arregula

el pié

llevar  todo

burnt

por la fuerza

2.                         la suerte

distritos convenientes

para

los que use

poder

mira

bajo

la mano

allow

a commissary of

the other; which

shall be                to

employ

se declara          que la guerra

destruye

## Article XXIII.

the United States

fe

limits

in quintuplicate

our Lord        en

Cuevas

{three}

# A Vigilance Committee of Jurors, a Mexican Lynching, 1848-present

the men

none brown

none kin

none you

gather at the tree

the newspaper omits

⌢

omittere
ob/mittere
toward/mission
toward/meith
toward/remove

the verdict

⌢

verdit
ver/dit
truth/saying

# Nopales, A Mexican Lynching, No. 39

*"Mexicans have no business in this country. I don't believe in them. The men were made to be shot at, and the women were made for our purposes. I'm a white man— I am! A Mexican is pretty near black. I hate all Mexicans."*
*- April 6, 1850, Stockton Times Op-Ed*

.a nopal could be weeping
      but who       examines
                        las espinas
     closely
as the blossoms                   .a fire
          quema todo
          pero salva
          los que cubren

                                      la llama


.a nopal could be quiet
      but who       plunges
                   each thorn
     into the drum

and swallows                    .the rust

        no es
        una cortina
        para parar

                  el torrente.


.a nopal could be asleep
      but who     kicks
          the hibernating
      until sunrise
shows               they are countless
        .the drought
        is rooted
        in birth

                    en una paciencia de ríos

# Framework

Not Knowing One's Place

The Penalty Of Retribution

PayingAttentionToWhiteWomenWalkingTowardOthersConflictOverLandCompetingWalkingDownStairs GivingRefugeToOutlawsFightingGiveAidToAnOutlawTheftBan

RefusingToPlayMusicForAnglos

JoteroBracero

Not Doing Your Job

"200 Most Respectable Citizens" forming the Committee of Vigilance

The accompanying figures are portraits of the native population in these districts; two of them are women in humble life, and the third is a porter carrying baggage across the Isthmus.

more orderly than we ever recollect

NATIVE WOMEN.    NATIVE PORTER.

dirtyTrainwreckingDrunksKillingAnglosCowThreateningToKillAnglos HerdingSheepBillCollectorsSellingCDsSellingLooseysF

Earning A Living

ProtestingShouting; VivaDiaz! WitchcraftAttemptingToPreventLynchingRefusingToCooperateWithVigilantesBreakingVigilanteVowOfSilenc

Court RidingInThePassengerSeatLivingOnYourLandUsingPhone

eProtestingTheKillingOfAMexicanEncouragingMexicanAnAnglo SupportingLove

### INTERIOR OF CALIFORNIA.

CERTAIN travellers who have visited California have reported the country to be strangely deficient in natural beauty, a statement which the accompanying View goes far to refute.

This scene has been sketched by our Correspondent near Russian River, 100 miles north-west of San Francisco. Within thirty miles, the country changes from the "oak plains" of Santa Rosa to the alpine scenery of this sketch. The land is equally rich; the game equally abundant; the climate, if possible, more beautiful. The red-wood pine predominates, but oak of a hardy description is not sparse; the wild grape and raspberry are very luxuriant; salmon and trout are plentiful; and the grizzly bears a little too numerous, if anything. This district, the "further back" (from the centre of civilisation), in fact populating. The rocks in the foreground of the Sketch contain 25 and 30 per cent. of gold; but, at present, the expense of working by machinery would not repay labour and cost. The scene of the Sketch is now the residence of an English gentleman, who blends cultivating as much of the surrounding soil as is practicable. The accompanying figures are portraits from the native population of this district; two of them are women in humble life, and the third is a porter carrying baggage across the Isthmus.

### THE FIRST PUBLIC EXECUTION AT SAN FRANCISCO.

LYNCH law was never carried into execution with greater deliberation and more solemnity than at San Francisco on last June 10th and 11th. A number of the most respectable citizens, not less than two hundred, being convinced, as they state in their "constitution," that "there is no security for life or property under the law as now administered," being much annoyed at the escape of some criminals, and the slow process of the law in regard to others, formed themselves, the day before that date, into a Vigilance Committee for the protection of life and property. They bound themselves by their honour to perform every lawful act for the maintenance of law and order, and to "sustain the law when faithfully and properly administered." They were determined, however, "that no thief, burglar, incendiary, or assassin shall escape punishment, either by the quibbles of the law, the insecurity of prisons, the carelessness or corruption of the police, or laxity of those who pretend to administer justice." The late fire, causing the destruction of the city, was generally attributed to incendiaries,

Certain travellers who have visited California have reported the country to be strangely deficient in natural beauty, a statement which the accompanying View goes far to refute.

LYNCH LAW IN CALIFORNIA.—SCENE OF THE FIRST EXECUTION IN SAN FRANCISCO, ON JUNE 10.

Lynch Law in California - Scene of the First Execution in San Francisco, on June 10

ToMarry RumorOfPastBeingThieves,Informers,Spies,AndMurderers MistakenForOutlawBeingADesperateCharacterDrivingTakingAngloTo Perception Word of Mouth

## La Sirena, a Mexican Lynching, after the hanging death of Josefa Segovia, Downieville, CA, July 5, 1851

Guilt is not
guilty is not
free is not
noose is not
jury is not
self is not
a defense is not
judge is not
verdict is not
appeal is not
the ways which
a miner
pans
and pans
and pans and
pans and
pans until
a fleck appears,
eventually
something
must be found,
eventually
someone must

Josefa is not
Juana is not
Juanita is not
an assembled
bridge of
independence
atop the
Yuba River now
court now
kangaroo now
noose
and song
left to walk
through left
to float
above left to
the treaty of
Guadalupe
Hidalgo and
how all men
are created
equal
until a border

67

let the blade
taste,
make,
tear
a seam,
a seam
uncooked is
the point in
which a man
spills red
from the white
heat glowing
and heaving until she
stops
him
until the town
claims siren,
claims capital.

born and
there is money
to be made
until man is not
laborer is
not woman is
not mexican is
not white is not
the moment
a town stops
to watch
a person
face
the crowd
and wrap a rope
around
the neck,
claims leap.

In the air flight is real is probable is the moment of weightlessness before the snap before the eye decides to untangle TheDarkTheOtherTheUnknown before the river parts and she kicks and kicks below until they say she is consumed until they accept silences until she dives with a deep breath of water the people accept her body thrashes beneath surface but this is not burial, this is a defiance, a KickingSingingKickingSinging chant.

# A Mexican Lynching by El Venado que ve nada, No. 45

"I am opposed to Capital Punishment in communities when they have prisons to keep murderers secure for life, but in new settlements, and new countries, like California where there is little or no protection from the hands of such monsters in human shape, it becomes necessary to dispose of them by the shortest mode, for the safety of the community."
- John Eagle, California gold miner, 1853, in a letter to his wife

graves:     named
            or unnamed
            still

            cloak bones;

skin:
flayed      split       shorn                           punctured

            flapping

asks of the vein for only so long;

                                                                                    scrotum:
                                                                                     relent
                                                                              to a boy kicking
                                                                                     the hung

                                                                 so hard

both testicles explode

                                                                 so hard

the noose goes mute

                                                                 so hard

an idle town turns over on the spine of a deer,        who bucks

                                        the people:
                               stay                                        static,
                               say:


hangthem*bringthecamera***haveapicnicinthisshadow***youarenotmyneighbor***buildafence***leavethesick***gowest***thislandismyland***wewillmakethisgreataga-*
*in*digagrave***buildawall***whathappenedtomyeyeswhathappenedtomyeyes***whathappenedtomyeyes*
*whathappenedtomyeyes***whathappenedtomyeye***swhathappenedtomyeyes*

the blood:
                        parts
armless,            without consent, diffuses earth,
          listens for the echo of the others,                accrues inside
                        a nearby well's aquifer,
pumps

]coffee cup[

anything can be

[trophy]

just as
anything can be

[ashtray]

]flower pot[

]witness[

claim
anything,
any thing

]the inside of

]curb[

]victim[

claim

]halo[

claim

your

another's    wrist[

]the quiet breath of a body at rest[

claim

]colony[

claim

]president[

claim

]horn[

claim

]vein[

claim

]badge[

claim

any thing

]cadaver[

claim

]coffin[

claim

72

# Artifacts on a Hanging Tree, Goliad, Texas (a series of 70 Mexican Lynchings, 1857)

"Site for court sessions at various times from 1846 to 1870. Capital sentences called for by the courts were carried out immediately, by means of a rope and a convenient limb. Hangings not called for by regular coursts occurred here during the 1857 "cart war" - a series of attacks made by Texas freighters against Mexican drivers along the Indianola-Goliad/San Antonion Road. About 70 men were killed, some of them on this tree, before the war was halted by Texas Rangers."
-State Historical Survey Committee Texas Marker near the tree

## Last 5 TripAdvisor Reviews of Goliad's Hanging Tree, as of 6/23/18

Title: Love old court houses (6/20/18)
Review: This hanging tree was just a bonus on the court house square and the history that took place there was moving.

Title: Spooky when you think of the tree's use! (6/18/18)
Review: One of the sites in Goliad is the hanging tree a beautiful tree which was used to mete out "justice" after trials.

Title: Beauty of a tree (6/19/18)
Review: Well the name sort of says it all, but that is a beautiful tree. The courthouse is a class Texas courthouse, so the day was great.

Title: Interesting in a gruesome kind of way (5/27/18)
Review: This is a huge oak tree outside of the courthouse in Goliad. You really can picture the sentences being carried out.

Title: Huge old live oak tree (5/7/18)
Review: The tree is located in the center of town on the grounds of the county courthouse. The tree has quiet the history. When convicted, the prisoner was walked outside and hanged from this magnificent live oak tree.

TalkToTheOakTree:AskTheCityToTearYouDown.CityFortifies WithStone.AskTownToGoIntoHiding.StateErectsMetalPlaque.AskTouriststoLeave. AndTheyTestYourStrengthToHoldTheirWeight.AskThemIf TheyNoticeYourShadow'sShapeIsAMassBurialOfTwitchingLegs.LetThemMemory.

## El árbol, No. 10, as a series of narrowing translations:

El que a buen árbol se arrima, buena sombra le cobija. |...| He who nears a good tree, is blanketed by good shade. |...| The one that comes to a good tree, good shadow blankets them. |...| To near the tree, receive a blanket of shadow. |...| To near the tree is to blanket yourself in darkness.

Elegy of Skin, in Kerosene & Mesquite, Antonio Rodríguez, November 3, 1920

The noise                                                                  you did not make

The swallow                                                         The swallow of flames

The Tongue                                                          it is said flames lick

How                                                                                    Lick

                                                                                            Lick

                                                                                            Lick

                                                                                            Lick

How                                                                         you are tasted

in                                                                                  from the outside

Rodriguez was arrested this morning when he applied at a ranch near Rock Springs for food. The mob began to form early in the afternoon, and by night several thousand persons had gathered. Later the crowd stormed the frail prison at Rock Springs, overpowered the guard, and took Rodriguez some distance from the city to an already prepared pyre.

*"It is so American, fire. So like us. / Its desolation. And its eventual, brief triumph"*
— Larry Levis, "My Story in a Late Style of Fire"

How
                    from the bottom,
up

How
                         satiation

How it is
your you, split


How it is to feel

How nothing

How it is to monument
the eyes

                    & you watch

                                        a pyre is satiated


                                        Western it is to forget


                                        to watch what was once

                                                            & peel
                                                            away

                                                        yourself less

                                                            goes numb


                                        waiting
                                        for your oblivion,
                                                    their unraveling

# MEXICAN MURDERER IS BURNED AT STAKE

*"Rodríguez struggled a few minutes, but never whimpered."*

- San Antonio Daily News, November 4, 1910

# Still Life as Incantation, after Antonio Gomez, a Mexican Lynching, June 19, 1911

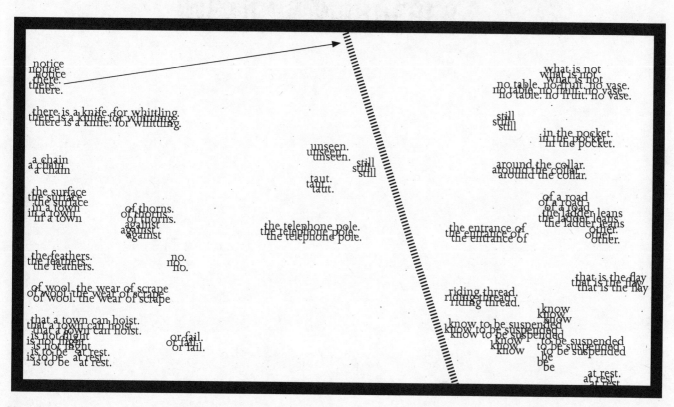

# Act III – Scene 2: After the Drowned who Leapt from the Mercurio, Operation Wetback, 1954

*The Justice Department permitted the Immigration Service to crowd 500 Mexicans aboard a ship that normally carried 70 to 90 persons.*
*- United Press, August 1956*

*(All in place. Lights up.)*

Unnamed Speaker 1 (*Downstage, facing audience, Standing*):
Choose        ::       as if choice appears when learning the last thing that disappears is the hair
             ::       the surface,
             ::       before the gulf     breathes

                ::         the others
                ::         in

Unnamed Speaker 2 (*Upstage, facing stage left, hunched, pacing*):
To remain       ::       is to grieve
             ::       is to answer
                ::         what side of the río
                           we crown
                ::         or
                ::         where your ancestors
                           coffin

Unnamed Speaker 3 (*center stage, laying prone, facing downstage*):
We spill  ::       from the deck
            ::        one heart after another after another after another after another after another after
                     another after another after another [repeat a total of 37 times] beating
            ::        on the waves


            ::        escape
            ::        is in the sinking


Unnamed Speaker 4 (*center stage, laying suppine atop Unnamed Speaker 3*):
To be willing    ::        to dive the core until sea water
                           boils
            ::        the lungs must be a church


                     ::        beyond breathing
                     ::        where a christ dies
                     ::        with each new moon


3 Additional Unknown Speakers (*Offstage, with each speaker starting once the prior has uttered "Her only ask"*):
Her only ask    ::        scaffold a new atlantis before sun-
            ::        rise


            ::        because the captors may ask, how much
            ::        to cage vermillion


                     (*Lights fade inward leaving center stage lit until blackout. Curtain.*)

# La Maceta, a Mexican Lynching, in 7 artifacts, No. 52

1. Daily Alta California, August 13, 1855, on Lynching

**Mob Law.**

The fell spirit of mob law is widely at work in the country. The horrible massacre at Rancheria, Amador County, has inflamed the public mind against the Mexican population, and a war of extermination is going on against them. No inquiry is made as to the guilt of one of the proscribed race, but they are hanged as unceremoneously as the huntsman shoots down the deer or the coyote

2. Ballot Summary of California Prop. 63[1] (1986), a fading

Provides that English is the official language of State of California. Requires Legislature to enforce this provision by appropriate legislation. Requires Legislature and **state** officials **to take all steps necessary to ensure** that the role of **English** as the common language of the state **is preserved** and enhanced. Provides that the Legislature shall make no law which **diminish**es or ignores the role of English as the common language. Provides that **any** resident of or **person** doing business in state shall have standing to sue the state to enforce these provisions.

3. Pete Wilson speaks on C-SPAN, November 1994 in support of Prop 187, the backbone of his gubernatorial campaign[2]

*"This has nothing to do with race"*

## 4. Ballot Summary of California Prop. 187[3] (1994) as a Triptych of Deduction

The People of California ██████████ | The People ███████████████████
███████████ are suffering ████ | ██████ have suffered █████████
hardship caused by the | ████████████████████████
██████████████████████ | presence ████████████████ is ██████
████████████████████ |
████████████████████ |
criminal conduct of ███████████ |
██████████████████████ |
██████ government ███ | ███ they have a right to ██ protection
███ entering ██████ unlawfully. | entering this country ████
████ the People of California declare ██ |
█████████████████████████ |
██████████████████ agencies ████ |
██████████████████████ | illegal ███████████████████

---

1. Prop 63 passed with the highest voter approval in the state's voter history: 74%, deemed symbolic.
2. Pete Wilson won his re-election effort with a 55% of voters in support.
3. Prop 187 passed with 59% of voters in support of denying all benefits to undocumented immigrants, including K-12 education and access to healthcare, ruled unconstitutional.

# A Request for Information: ICE - Regarding Immigration Detention Services Expansion, 2017
## (Chicago, St. Paul, Detroit, Salt Lake City)

1) Definitions and Terms

Source:

[Multiple]: consisting of, including, or involving more than one

[Possible]: having an indicated potential

[Potential]: expressing possibility

[Detention]: a holding in custody

[Custody]: immediate charge and control (as over a ward or a suspect) exercised by a person or an authority

[Control]: to have power over the other

[Power]: possession of control, authority, or influence over others

[Possession]: the act of having or taking into control

[Control]: to have power over the other

"Multiple Possible Detention Sites To Hold Criminal Aliens and Other Immigration Violators"

2) Clarifications:

Figure 1:          "Appropriate Strategies"

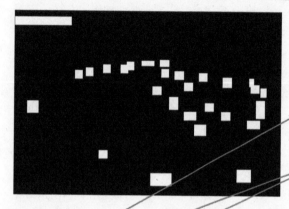

"To Obtain Market Information . . .
For Planning Purposes and Determine
Appropriate Strategies to Meet the Agency's
Requirements"

"The Government Will Not Pay for Any
Information"

"ICE is Responsible for the Detention of
Individuals in Removal Proceedings and Who
are Amenable to Removal from the US"

In the absence
of information,                    the evidence
                                        of absence

                    cites erasure.

Removal –Read as 'expulsion, deportation, void,
homogeneity, violence, expendable, or_____"

Amenable – Read as 'viable for removal'

3) Legal Guidance:

Plessy vs. Ferguson (1896) Ruling by U.S. Supreme Court:

"███ consider the underlying fallacy ████████████████
in the assumption ███████████████████ of ███████████████
████████████████████████████████████████████

█████████████████████████████ the Constitution of the
United States can██ put them upon the same plane."

"Facilities Shared with other
Detained Populations Will Be
Considered as long as Appropriate
Separation"

4) Visual Definitions:

Figure 2 - Maximum

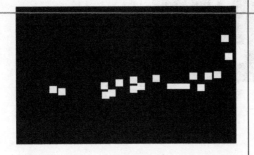

"The Ideal Facility or Facilities Will
Provide Minimum, Medium and
Maximum Security"

Figure 3 - Medium

Figure 4 - Minimum

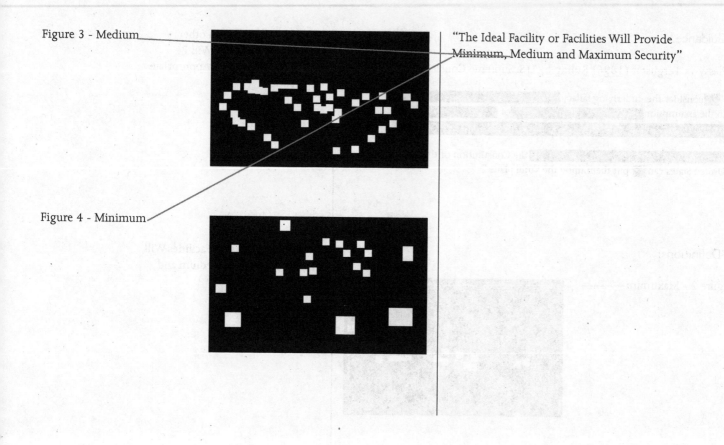

"The Ideal Facility or Facilities Will Provide Minimum, Medium and Maximum Security"

## 5) The De-Escalation of Human

::Human::                    ::Man::                    ::Fallible::
          ::Earth-
bound::              ::Weak::              ::Someone::
::Some-
body::                    ::Anybody::                    ::Any-
thing::
                                                    ::Thing::
          ::Stuff::
                    ::Matter::

::Material::                    ::Resource::
                                        ::Replace-
                                        able::

               ::Product::

          ::Value::                              ::Cost
::Sale::
               ::Revenue::

                                        ::Profit::

"The Government has priced detention contracts with an all-in bed day rate. Are there other pricing structures that could be used to better distribute risk between the Government and a Contractor, which might result in better operational and business outcomes for all parties?"

## 6) Supporting Data and Projections

Figure 5 - Chart:  "Revenue Potential" Revenue and Acceptable Level of Deaths"

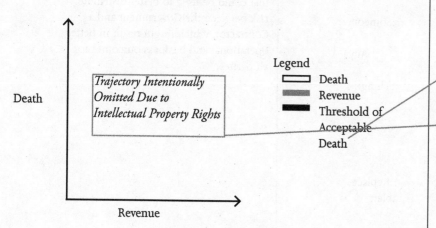

Death

Trajectory Intentionally
Omitted Due to
Intellectual Property Rights

Legend

☐ Death
▬ Revenue
▬ Threshold of Acceptable Death

Revenue

"The Government has various requirements for operations at its facilities. Based on your experience, which of these requirements drive the most cost? Why? Are there any changes to requirements that you might recommend that would better meet 'best value' -- i.e., by reducing cost substantially without sacrificing the effectiveness of core operations?"

"Does the Contractor have any innovative ideas for leveraging technology, data, or analytics in order to decrease costs or increase staff efficiency in detention facilities? Please briefly describe."

Figure 6 - Chart:   "Profit Maximization" Number of Rapid
Deportations and Profit Potential

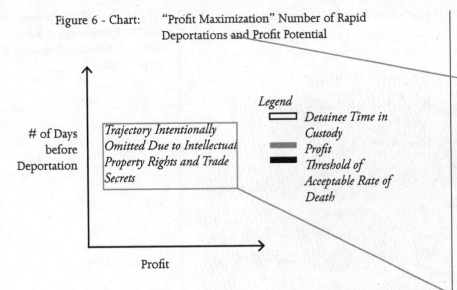

# of Days
before
Deportation

*Trajectory Intentionally Omitted Due to Intellectual Property Rights and Trade Secrets*

*Legend*

☐ *Detainee Time in Custody*
▬ *Profit*
▬ *Threshold of Acceptable Rate of Death*

Profit

"The Government would like to work with its Contractors to jointly identify, plan, prioritize, and implement cost improvement initiatives throughout the period of performance. What experience does your company have in such activities? Briefly describe both your internal cost improvement capabilities and how you work with other enterprises (e.g., your customers or suppliers) to enact joint improvements."

"Does the Contractor have any innovative ideas for leveraging technology, data, or analytics in order to decrease costs or increase staff efficiency in detention facilities? Please briefly describe."

"If you are unable to comply with ICE 2011 Performance-Based National Detention Standards, What would it take?"

# El Arpa, a Mexican Lynching, No. 53

*"The office of sheriff is a critical part of the Anglo-American heritage of law enforcement. We must never erode this historic office."*
*-Jeff Sessions, former U.S. Attorney General, February 12, 2018 to the National Sheriffs' Association*

1. The inheritance of the heir is never a dandelion disbursal. Scattershot. Floating beyond fences. Growing elsewhere.

2. The inheritance of the elsewhere is a cave of collapse.

3. The cave of collapse is work.

4. The work is never inheritance of the heir's or of the heir's heir, as well as the heir's heir's heir.

5. The inheritance of repetition is a soundless gavel buried in a shallow grave.

6. The shallow grave is the redness of the bouquet a florist selects.

7. The bouquet is a leaning into the quiet of a funeral.

8. The quiet of a funeral is the Americas.

9. The Americas is a platform, built by the settlers, sheriffs, and miners, for the lynching of the other.

10. The lynching is in a vigilance committee of NAFTA, Operation Wetback, Maquiladoras, ICE, silences, the agricultural prison industrial complex, congressmen, and US presidents.

11. The silences is a gerrymandering of census data.

12. The census data is learning about the word incarceration through the storytelling project playing on public radio.

13. The incarceration is an ombligo of shirts in a forest of screams.

14. The ombligo is feeding again and never hungry.

15. The feeding is a church of excommunications inside a cage of teeth.

16. The cage of teeth is elected into office.

17. The elected are voting to eliminate whatever and everything.

18. The voting are no longer asking permission.

19. The permission is trafficking.

20. The trafficking is now asked to self-report.

21. The self-report is now asked to fill out a binary form in ink, online.

22. The binary is seeking a fourth option during the election.

23. The election is a wall.

24. The wall is a type of silence.

25. The silence is a type of America.

26. The type of America is in the arrest.

27. The arrest is defined as the cessation or stoppage of motion.

28. The cessation or stoppage of motion is the fabric veiling the artifice.

29. The fabric veiling the artifice is a factory of harps.

30. The factory of harps is a maker of a stringless harp.

31. The stringless harp is the mute progeny.

32. The mute progeny is now the inheritance of the heir.

# Self Portrait: Upon Viewing My Own Crime Scene, a Mexican Lynching

I have imagined
a corpse.
imagined
myself
many times.
This is not
bleak,
or surprising,

in pieces.
Strangers have
me split many more times
than
less

digging,
for a window.

Learn
I carry.
Forget the type

myself
I have

a corpse

new,

strangers
have imagined me

imagined

I have. And they know
about me. That the Gone
are inside,
hungry
I flip through
my police file.
the type of blood

I stopped

pumping. See
I mud.

watch myself.


Wants and wants.
It is always a man.
to the dead
of my left ear, asleep

How it is
when the body commits
hold the image near.
nothing of
tire tracks and shuffle
the paperwork
statements
Where were you?
form. No mouth or

I have heard
the sound of
the vacuumed
and drowned

when I spill,
The policeman
watches me
Wants to
know how
I ended.
I say
He does not listen
and he turns to a photo
on a palm
frond.
to fall apart,
and
I say
the noose, hoof prints,

and find no witness
to my own nest of limbs.
I cannot speak to this
tongue. Burnt sockets
are no home for sight.

my throat,

a night wind. I was there.

no space
the moon is a city
which my body strung

is the cradle of wasps
in a field,
patient   until

now


I saw nothing. I see
to write – sometimes
on
wrath. Sometimes
the body
humming
forgotten,
the nearing
and the frenzy,
none sleep.

# Bracero(s) & The Ice Car

I.

The circumference
of a town                          is a proverb.

II.

How distant the railroad tracks bisect                                    the people

                                                                                      & the possessor
                from the center to create            the corporeal.

III.

That distance is Bracero(s)

                              in the ice car                    all day

            stacking

            & loading & replenishing                 the cold

                                                      the ice

                                                      all day.

IV.

In the proximity   is the burn

            of Bracero(s),              a slow    freeze

                        into the ice car

                        into the summer
                        into this land & that.

V.

Draw the circle.

Ask Bracero(s):                   : Do you have an alien registration number?

      Reduce the radius, & redraw.

Ask Bracero(s):                   : Can you recite the pledge of allegiance?

      Reduce the radius, & redraw.

Ask Bracero(s):                   : Where are you living at present?

      Reduce the radius, & redraw.

Ask Bracero(s):                   : Who is the father of America?

      Reduce the radius, & redraw.

Ask Bracero(s):                   : Are there children?

      Reduce the radius, & redraw.

Ask Bracero(s):                    : Are you married?

    Reduce the radius, & redraw.

Ask Bracero(s):                    : Where did you enter this country?

    Reduce the radius, & redraw.

Ask Bracero(s):                    : Do you have family on the other side?

    Reduce the radius, & redraw.

Ask Bracero(s):                    : Does sensation remain in your fingertips?

    Reduce the radius, & redraw.

Ask Bracero(s):                    : Can you sign your full name inside this box?
    Reduce the radius, & redraw.

VI.

To narrow a body, excise.

How to Lynch a Mexican (1848 - Present) *

*When possible, the poem should be read simultaneously by 4 readers, or in groups of 4, with each reader or group picking a different direction to read.

Call a Mexican to their door and shoot a Mexican.

Hang a Mexican during interrogation.

Beat a Mexican and drag a Mexican by buggy.

Shoot a Mexican with a mob of 200 men.

Shoot a Mexican and let a Mexican rot.

Shoot a Mexican, decapitate a Mexican, tie a Mexican to a tree log, and throw a Mexican into the river.

Take a Mexican from a hospital and hang a Mexican.

Shoot a Mexican and leave a Mexican.

A mishap happens to a Mexican on the way to jail.

Tie wire around a Mexican neck, drag a Mexican, and shoot a Mexican.

Capture a Mexican, transport a Mexican, and shoot a Mexican.

Take a Mexican from a Mexican village to the hillside and execute a Mexican.

Take a Mexican from jail, beat a Mexican, and secretly bury a Mexican.

Shoot a Mexican in front of a Mexican wife.

Find a Mexican with a gun shot in a Mexican head and drag a Mexican off.

Disappear a Mexican.

Lose a Mexican.

---

Hang a Mexican.

Whip a Mexican.

Shoot a Mexican with a gun.

Shoot a Mexican with a rifle.

Lash a Mexican 75 times, then hang a Mexican.

Beat a Mexican, then hang a Mexican.

Hang a Mexican from a Live Oak.

Construct a platform over a river, apply the noose on a Mexican on the platform, and tell a Mexican to leap.

Overpower the deputy to seize a Mexican from the courthouse, drag a Mexican by horse to a tree, hang a Mexican.

Abduct a Mexican from a Mexican home and hang a Mexican.

Abduct a Mexican from a Mexican home while they are sleeping and hang a Mexican.

Hang a Mexican with a log-chain.

Tie a Mexican to a mesquite tree, pour kerosene on a Mexican, and light a Mexican on fire, do not shoot a Mexican.

Bind a Mexican, then decapitate a Mexican.

---

Pound a Mexican head in and hang a Mexican inside a courtroom.

Mutilate a Mexican, shoot a Mexican, and drag a Mexican.

Burn a Mexican.

Form a vigilance committee and hang a Mexican from a windmill.

Shoot a Mexican and cut off each ear of a Mexican.

Hang a Mexican in broad daylight.

Hang a Mexican under the cover of night.

Hang a Mexican in front of a crowd.

Hang a Mexican from a telephone poll.

Hang a Mexican after a mock trial.

Execute a Mexican with a posse.

Hang a Mexican from a bridge.

Drag a Mexican down main street.

Hang a Mexican until a Mexican is freed and a Mexican goes back to jail and go back to the jail and take a Mexican to the nearest tree, and hang a Mexican.

Lash a Mexican 300 times, then hang a Mexican.

Decapitate a Mexican and pickle a Mexican head in a jar.

Torture a Mexican and hang a Mexican.

Torture a Mexican.

Drag a Mexican down main street and hang a Mexican.

Take a Mexican from a steamboat and hang a Mexican from the yard-arm of the dock.

Hang a Mexican, then burn the corpse of a Mexican.

Burn a Mexican alive.

Hang a Mexican indiscriminately.

Put on masks to take a Mexican from authorities and hang a Mexican.

Hang a Mexican, then shoot a Mexican.

Hang a Mexican, then shoot a Mexican in a Mexican face.

Round up a Mexican, round up a Mexican, round up a Mexican, hang a Mexican, hang a Mexican, and hang a Mexican.

Beat a Mexican with a club.

Shoot a Mexican in the back of a Mexican head.

Find a Mexican at a dance and shoot a Mexican.

See a Mexican on the road and shoot a Mexican.

Capture a Mexican and cut a Mexican throat with an axe.

Trample a Mexican with a horse.

Slice a Mexican throat.

Seize a Mexican, take a Mexican to a river, shoot a Mexican, and throw a Mexican into the river.

Kill a Mexican and feed a Mexican to hogs.

Shoot a Mexican with a mob of 20 men.

Shoot a Mexican in jail.

{four}

front

# The Things Fed to Fire Return

Every sunrise
The things fed

                    to

                                                       since a distant snow.
                                                       fire return.

Innocuous at first:
               shriveled
                     A vinyl

who'd forgotten speech,

                                                       Two siblings

     listen
         to the garble
& scratch.
                                                           put on the record,

                    They draw
                    a new sacred
                                            each shriek into

no one can read.
                                                        text
                                                        No one learned.

The last
takes
a rocking chair,
                                         dog
      a quiet
                                                         the wood
                                                                 crumble.

torso

                              twisted, head-
                              less
                              at the courthouse
                              all wait

for the lynched.

A mannequin

perches
&

A cremated schoolteacher
returns.

               Intact.

                            Lifeless.
                        The things fed
                             return.

to fire
Every sunrise
          a new wrath.

a new dread,

# Ojo

You claim

*eyes
are the windows
to the soul.*

Instead          apply the paper bag

test.                    Fortunate skin. You

pass          the tattered exam-

ination. And you think

about the hazel iris.                    How

it enters          .          quiet, shifts

colors with a coat,

blends          to mask          tones. Matches.

You

are reminded

of this:

the neighbor of a northern

California mass shooter says

*he had blue eyes, but I*
*swear they went dark.*

And slip through

        street              after street,

      rooms in a home that is not yours

           but your father built.             Moving

                            along. To never make

         contact.

                  You know someone will ask

of tongue

or of blood.

Know the ancestors hunger to noose the branches of the other.

Do not

linger.                  Pass. And pass. And pass through and

forward and on and inside and

              when you finally

                                    distance,

question the severed head
of Murrieta, now
pickled, if the mob                     asked            how
                                        the roundness of a retina
                                        remains a constant.

He does not blink, says:

                                                                        *they fed the mountain*
                                                                        *the coal and the forest*
                                                                        *the timber but no one*
                    *eyed the core. It hungered deeply. And*            *it did not want stone.*

114

# Searching

Perhaps a weeping cactus speaks

in the pancreas of all fauna.

Perhaps everyone listens, gathers

in an apse of echo.

Perhaps the center of main now

of carcasses create eclipse.

in a desert town: the names of the soon slain rest

their dogs, unyokes the oxen, and bundles the sparrows

cleaves a river of coagulation, and the pile

Perhaps, in the absence,

a kingdom of mirrors.

each person rummages the innards for the forgotten and discovers

Perhaps each reflection births

shudders and crumbles.

a howl so shrill that each root, mountain, and river hears,

Perhaps,

remains.

a cactus

# The Desert is Circular, To Escape, Spiral

Wander.

SUEÑO.
SONIDO.
CICATRIZ.

Everything                    emotion
or anguish.
   Nature vessels.

SUEÑO.
SONIDO.
CICATRIZ.

                    The ventricles.

                                        Sand.

                    The kidneys.

                                        Smoke.

SUEÑO.
SONIDO.
CICATRIZ.

                    The bones.

                                        Ash.

                    And the lungs.

                                        Thickets.
                                        Thorns.

SUEÑO.
SONIDO.
CICATRIZ.

At dusk, igneous vibrates
and kindles
      to remind when passing my shadowself,

                                            for the third
                                and       fourth time,

      Consider Satan

made man

         in his image.

SUEÑO.
SONIDO.
CICATRIZ.

117

SUEÑO.
SONIDO.
CICATRIZ.

The living        believe
    the theory of                language is
                the younger a person is
                the easier it is
                        to acquire

    a second tongue.
Yet:

                Ask the recently buried
                and the carcassed
how to tongue

                silence amid
                flames.        But
                        the only sound is
                        parchment
      collapse.
                Ask
     how to repair
     a nervous
                  system
                  with a swallowed horizon
                  and silt.        And
                    hear echoes.
Do
not ask
         why voice                erupts
            bilingual,
like you.

SUEÑO.
SONIDO.
CICATRIZ.

EÑO.
NIDO.
ATRIZ.

SUEÑO.
SONIDO.
CICATRIZ.

SUEÑO.
SONIDO.
CICATRIZ.

SUEÑO.
SONIDO.
CICATRIZ.

Be passenger

strapped to the roof
on a broken railway.
Hurtling
jungles, serpentines,
and the invented.

Shout to Conductor,

have you seen me
before?

SUEÑO.
SONIDO.
CICATRIZ.

And if so,
where do the ancestors
corral?
Ask Conductor,
if        he can stop,
or

find you

space

below.

SUEÑO
SONID
CICAT

O.
O.
RIZ.

Tell the self;

                                        *it is not*

*an oasis.*  But

                                             a voice from inside earth
repeats,

*Love the mirror.*
*Love the mirror.*
*Love the mirror and free*

                                             *the yoke.*

            Few believe tectonic plates
            have                     ears.

A person should.
     And answer
      *Yes.*

            The below would respond:

                                          *In the desert*
                                          *was the end.*

       *And*

                  *in the end,*
                  *a spiral.*

SUEÑO.
SONIDO.
CICATRIZ.

# A [Disintegrated] Portrait of God, as a Border

The kingdom        [closed]

[Imagined]

[you]
at the gates
but never noticed
signs                    [exit only]

In the corner

a child

asks

*Where is [entrance]?*
*Where is [mother]?*
*Where is my [throat]?*

[Imagined]          [you]          mouth
answers
space to breathe

[You] point

               lineate
               pew
               forgive
               exult
               carry
               cross


          others    [exist]

barbed wire [say]
you [swallow] the young

brick [say]
the old cannot [return] to cactus

mountain [say]
[kneeling] is just another way to keep still

river [say]
[return]

desert [say]
you built [this]     you [built] this     [you] built this

unborn [say]
[go]

dead [say]
[screaming] can also be called breath

you [say]
[                    ]

# Looped Instruction with Unimagined Boundary

curl into the sternum
    of a pig    of a lake    of a dream

    *blade smaller*

        of a hummingbird

rest your head
    near the aorta

        *listen*

        the fury of living

    trembles
*listen*
    dissolves
    a border
    the spirits

    walk through
    or    walk away

                    and the rib-
cage-                                    splayed-
open                                     wings

                    when pressed


    once                      there was flight

yes    once
       you dropped
       into a cactus
                                                  a tunneldredge from dark

            found a mirror
            and called the mirror
            other              obscured the hand inviting entrance
                               curl into the sternum

126

# The Axolotl Speaks

*You can cut the spinal cord, crush it, remove a segment, and it will regenerate. You can cut the limbs at any level—the wrist, the elbow, the upper arm—*
*and it will regenerate, and it's perfect. There is nothing missing, there's no scarring on the skin at the site of amputation, every tissue is replaced.*
*They can regenerate the same limb 50, 60, 100 times. And every time: perfect.*
*- Scientific America, April 2011*

Tu me dices: you are losing       the animal
within.      Y yo digo nada.     How can you
battle             a diety. Instead I ask,
                      how many

times        have you offered
                your arms?

How many?
    How
    do you
    describe
           infinite.

70
x 7.
The nervous system.        Transmutations. Re-calibrated.

                                    Spine.
                                    Re-
                                    stacked.

Eres guardia?       Or guarded?
And you welcome
                                                        silence
with            space,                      with            quiet.
        So I must consider
your revival alone:             the monstrance
opening.
And my tied             tongue   to knees.
                        Enséñame.
Undeed this     border.
                Make me
explain         Xochimilco,

                                canaled.
Nunca                                   libre.
Brain           clipped.
        Dolor.
A synapse                       lodged
between dendrites:

            una viuda, a retina, nulo, todo, a trucing fissure, a wand.
                        Olvidado
es el hueso.
        A chip, abandoned.             You finally say,
Do this

                in memory of me.

As if      I        could
           tragar un lago

                              and the cortex could

           steed,
                     spear,
and        war
           the       blood.
Then
you ask me:                 what remains
                            cuando has
                            deshecho
                            scars and reconstruiste
                            the self?
                            Gruñidos.
                            Yes. Growls.
                            Or simply,
                            virga gathering
                            in drought.

# No te quedes

No. Do not stay here. Along this on-ramp.
This hill. This earbone of blood, a puddled

      cochlea. No. A tectonic. No. An erupting contraption
      rugiendo until the manufactured labyrinth of trenzas

and nerves buckle and bridge. Somehow
las raíces florecen, the quiet exhale of soil

      resting from rain: la tierra nunca abandons, remains
      out of breath from farewells. Despedidas and patience

from a guidance of stars. No. Do not stay
here. Unleaf each tree. Deberry each bush.

      Satchel the ancestral and lagrimas. And board. Or walk.
      O mantienes. Or by holding your breath in such silence

that the deaf are startled. Until landing. Until
crossing. Hasta que puedes desaparacer between

      pasture and escalator. Until all and none know
      your people. Until you find yourself preparing

to merge onto a grey highway. Cement comes
from imploding the core. This is how they build

       from nothing: vaciando todo. But know everything
       remains: an unknown pile of repurposed meaning.

Beneath: a mastodon que se rindío. A split sequoia.
A shuttered village. A volcano of home que se aguarda.

       Que resuena. That counts the hairs en su tobillo. Notice
       the light is green. No. No te quedes. Go and know nebulas.

# Notes from Discarded

*after the photograph "Ojos Para Volar, Coyoacán, Mexico, 1991" by Graciela Iturbide*

                                                           Birds fetal at doors
                                                           in dark. No instruction.

                                                                   Plume. Cold.
                                                                      missed

Quiet

                                                           while thresholding. A child
                                                           each, till Grandmother scolds.

               will cradle

                                                           Never contact the lifeless.
                                                                       A child

                    will run,                                                        tell the Blind.
                                                                                Here are my friends.

                                                                                 They are sleeping.
                                                                                          A child

                                                                                         will run.
            Leave the found.                                                       Unsighted root.

                                                                                   Take up the two
                              stones.                                                 Apply them.

                                                                                   Stare skyward.
                                                                                             See.

                                                                                      Not forever.
                                                                                      Turn black,

        A moment of blue.                                                              darker. Lay
                                                                             on another doorstep.
                                        vision
                                                                              Listen to the traffic
                                                                                     of silences.

# Eating Migas

for Carmen Giménez Smith and Roberto Tejada

The anvil of my ear believes
We have ordered insect.

I project hormiga in Texas,
Large bloated delectable

Without fear of a thorax
Collapse raising a galaxy

Of crumbs, or a raindrop
Currenting diente

Labyrinth the throat.
A resurrection of ant.

Bootstomp. Fire.
Flood. Insecticide.

The erasure is jaula.
A pendulum,

A slow rattle
Racked in situ.

The architecture
Is in the mandible.

Comemos las migas
But we never talk

Of meal. Sabemos
Que cada cosa

Cambia cuando
Queremos creer.

This is how
We eat. Yes.

How ancient
The ant. Complicit

tangling of flame.
Equipped to consume

And stridulate. Unknown
populous. A scrutiny

To antennae the semblance
Of molecule. Of meat.

# Nightjars

> &gt; Nightjars know     this land

burns
and rebuke nest.

trays kindle, and observe

yards, raisin paper-

how fog is just a patient

fence for the worker.

> &gt; Nightjars see tinseled vine-

> &gt; Nightjars refuse

breathmechanicsfirmament
god   man

>

      trill    murmuration,
            distraction.
            consumption
                  silence.           Cite

                  of flight         the immolation
                                    of sky.

                                                    Nightjars

                                                  Cease
                                                  to offer

                                                  discovery

>   Nightjars say

                            treaties & trails & migrations

                            lend-lease

                            this had a name,

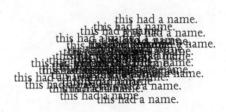

137

# Taking everything back

"In consideration of the extension acquired by the boundaries of the United States, as defined in the fifth article of the present treaty, the Government of the United States engages to pay to that of the Mexican Republic the sum of fifteen millions of dollars."
*Article XII of The Treaty of Guadalupe Hidalgo*

in the ever-

song

of the post-
now

:glassmortar crumb

to the switchgrass

:a molded man-
                                        myth of ioncumulus

        beneath the foot
                                        flame-




                                        praisedances
        a kingdom of
                rootmountainwormtierra




        to distance                     dirt.
                                        from
                                        dirty

to resyntax


the light

                                                as cradlingtenacious




:a prairie births itself,                                           absorbs made-


man

in leisure,


polishes rapture,



leans,




leans
unrushed

into
repose

# Instructions on How to Build the Morning, Tonight

[                                                    ]₁
I do not request a valley.
[                                                    ]₁
I bury the monument.

[                                                    ]₂
A campesino's son collapsing a sky blue ford pinto.
[                                                    ]₂
How I look toward the sun at setting, ignoring my retina.

[                                                    ]₃
My grandmother's left ventricle is weak.
[                                                    ]₃
In my neighborhood the dogs only want to fight.

[          ]<sub>4</sub>
  [          ]<sub>1</sub>

---

[1]To set everything on fire.
[2]Shape my back ampersand and fold. fold.
[3]While the shatter of my ojos is the origin of quiet.
[4]I tell the children of el futuro pasado, exhale.

## Cura for Surviving Drought

Be born.

Coyote

San Joaquin
sans
water this central.

this valley.

Fog

that                              gulps

Coyote

concretes.

a quick
sand

& gulps.

this

The mirage
is in the emptiness. Or

valley.

Orchards
thirst

                                                            until
                                                          drowned.

Almonds & blood
oranges

                                                Coyote

                                        Child

                            coughing

                                        & after-
                                           birth.

                    claws the hardpan,

dust

                    A cloud


themselves



ferment,


spill.
                                                this
                                              valley.

drags
itself
from womb,


Mother looks away,
                                          howls.


                                          tremors.

# Cura for Exhaustion via Mirror

Tell me

I mask

} how many days I unable to remain stone.

Tell me I am

I mask

} backward and upside down.

Tell me about

I mask

} my own ways.

Tell me a cathedral is not

I mask

} my desert bones.

Tell me my ancestors are not

    I mask  } the astral-winged.


Tell me to kindle

    I mask  } agave prayers and swaddled ash.


Tell me a canyon is not

    I mask  } a space for me to fortress.


Tell me I have

    I mask  } no mask.

Tell me you don't know
}
I mask     the shape of my grandmother's back.

Tell me to remove
}
I mask     this mask.

Tell me I do not see
}
I mask     you from behind the mask.

Tell me to forget
}
I mask     how my grandfather's memory lives in the spine of the whip.

Tell me the crevice is  
} no place to garden heartbeats.  
I mask


Tell me you do not hear  
} the nearing echo of veins.  
I mask

# Borderland Apocrypha

If your father tells you, and your teacher tells
      You, and the pastor at your family's church tells

You to perceive breath for existing, heart for source,
      Grave as final, voice as kingdom, and the shaking

As the escape of the earth's heat: you believe
      The repetition. But don't. Believe that earthquakes

Are fed by the buried, shoulders leaning in and sinewed
      By the unseen, combative to covert. Recall that beneath

You, nothing is still. Recall that beneath you, are the others.
      Know there is no such thing as living. Living is a birth

To control you, to fear no longer being present, to fear this,
      *Whatever your this is*, can leave you. The night's knuckle

On your door is not consent, but a decay of the ego,
      Unheard. A nearness unknown until an apnea arrives,

Tearing you from bed for the noose, the blade, the bullet,
      The fingers forcing the larynx. You were never living.

Your father will never tell you. The priest and prophet,
       And the succulent on the windowsill will not stop you, and

Say, you are not living. *You are present.* Some tomorrow,
       There will be no sunrise. None will say, where is?, where is?,

Where is?. They will believe you are no longer. Your blood
       Will mourn. The other will gather to publicly demonstrate,

Life is proprietary. Do not listen. Join the present at the tectonic
       And continue to be. *Push.* Press your ear against the mantle

To hear the sound of the pavement's rupture. *Push.* The city
       Will not sleep. *Push.* The flora fauna stone nod, you have

Always been present. *Push.* A valley is quiet whether cradling
       Or culling. *Push.* The television and the paper will say the fault

Is active. *Push.* The scientists will diagram the earth, halved,
       And demonstrate why nothing remains static. *Push.* The present

Remain, here. *Push.* Here. *Push.* Here. *Push.* Leave. Return.
       You exist. *Push.* You are present. *Push.* Swallow them into quiet.

# Acknowledgments

Unceasing praise to the editors of the following publications in which versions of these poems first appeared:

*The Boiler Journal*: "Nopales, a Mexican Lynching, No. 39" and "No te quedes"

*Gulf Coast*: "Searching"

*Ninth Letter*: "Elegy of Skin, in Kerosene & Mesquite, Antonio Rodríguez, November, 3, 1910" and "Standing in line to take a passport photo, an old white man looks at me and claims I am running"

*Puerto del Sol*: "Bracero(s) & The Ice Car"

*Tinderbox*: "The Axolotl Speaks"

*ctrl + v journal*: "Standing here because my grandpa ran away from home to sell perfume en el Zócalo at 9"

~

Nothing happens without the support of movements, community, family, and ancestors. Deep admiration, love, and respect to:

The Yokut, Mono, Washoe, Peoria, Potawatomi, and Miami peoples, on whose occupied territory I have lived, been nourished by, as well as on which I wrote this collection.

My mother for her love and generosity, my father for letting me roam, Joseph for being a shared heart with the same ferocity to dig for more, Jennie for showing me how to hustle, Mary and Michael for being blood and sharing in the halferness, Jacob for being down for whatever and always, Bernardo, Nichiren, Jennifer, Daniel, and Dena (of El Taller Latino Americano) for making NYC my second home, Russell for being imaginary, Josué for showing me the capacity of the spirit, and my grandparents who navigated imagined borders, The Bracero Program, wars, crossings, and the Dust Bowl to arrive at this moment.

The Hmong American Writers' Circle, my first poetry community in Fresno, who nourish and hold me, now and in my leanest years of writing: Andre Yang, Khaty Xiong, Ying Thao, Burlee Vang, Soul Vang, Pos Moua, Yia Lee, Mary Yang, Yashi Lee, Xai Lee, May Yang, Tony Vang, and Gao Yang, none of this is even possible without each of you.

CantoMundo and the founders Norma E. Cantú, Deborah Paredez, Celeste Guzmán Mendoza, Carmen Tafolla, and Pablo M. Martínez, you created a place in which I could find home inside of myself and in friendship with other Latinx Poets continue to ground me: Eduardo C. Corral, Ángel Garcia, Rosebud Ben-Oni, Javier Zamora, Vanessa Villarreal, Lupe Mendez, Natalie Scenters-Zapico, Ruben Quesada, Erika L. Sanchez, Emily Pérez, David Tomas Martinez, Leticia Hernández-Linares, Marcelo Hernandez Castillo, Denice Frohman, Manuel Paul López, Yesenia Montilla, Malcom Friend, Carolina Ebeid, Urayoán Noel, Ire'ne Lara Silva, Oscar Bermeo, Raina J. León, Lauren Espinoza, Andres Cerpa, Jasminne Mendez, Michael Luis Dauro, Amy Sayre Baptista, Diana Delgado, Emmy Pérez, José Antonio Rodríguez, Suzi F. Garcia, Francisco Aragón, Benjamin Garcia, Florencia Milito, Juan Luis Guzmán, and each and every CantoMundista I have not listed or met. We are family, we are growing. And to the faculty, Rigoberto Gonzalez, Roberto Tejada, Sandra Maria Esteves, Willie Perdomo, Aracelis Girmay, and Valerie Martínez for asking me to push.

The Community of Writers, especially the generous faculty of Sharon Olds, Evie Shockley, Kazim Ali, Mónica de la Torre, and Robert Hass, as well as a lifelong friend from the mountain in Keith S. Wilson. Each of you were part of the first group of people to see and hear the final phases of this collection, your kindness and willingness to navigate the work helped me in the last stretch of assembling this collection.

Toni Rudd my first teacher and boss in college. The first woman of color educator in my life who smiled when I told her I wrote poems and continues to be a guiding compass for how I move through my life.

The Fresno Poets who have come before me, created space, and shown me that a poor mixed kid from southeast Fresno could have the audacity to write a poem, perhaps even a collection of poems: Andrés Montoya, Ernesto Trejo, Luis Omar Salinas, Margarita Robles Luna, Larry Levis,

Mireyda "Mia" Barraza Martinez, Lawson Fusao Inada, Philip Levine, Marisol Baca, Tim Z. Hernandez, David Campos, Joseph Rios, Lee Herrick, Mas Masumoto, Sara Borjas, and more, many more.

The faculty and staff at Fresno State's MFA Program, as well as my colleagues and co-conspirators in and around the program and the Laureate Lab Visual Wordist Studio: J.J. Hernandez, Paul Sanchez, Raphique Barakat, Rebeca Flores, Jackie Huertaz, Erika Ceballos, Esmeralda Gamez, Javier Lopez, Jer Xiong, Chevas Clements, Angel Gonzalez, Emmanuel Mayoral, Rodolfo Avelar, and Mariah Bosch for your generosity in listening, collaborating, and pushing against the margin.

The #BlackLivesMatter movement, a necessary movement that continues the truth telling against erasures, violences, and sanctioned murders in the modern era. Lynching is in the framework of this nation; without continued efforts to support the movement, systemic issues will continue to end innocent lives without repercussions.

Mei-mei Berssenbrugge for peering into this collection, finding its spirit, and echoing the urgency and the histories that continue to be uttered into this land.

Rusty, Ken, Trisha, Gillian, and the Omnidawn Publishing team for your passion, belief in this collection, and ability to compress and expand the contents of my mind into a tangible object.

Juan Felipe Herrera and Carmen Giménez Smith, my longest mentors, teachers, and now friends – you have both cracked open my brain, hallucinated me into something better than I thought I was capable of becoming, and shown me corazónes I hope to emulate and radiate outward and forever.

To all the poets and writers who have held space for me for even a brief moment along these many paths, I cannot list you all, but I see you, and am better because of you.

And, Mai Der Vang, I am humbled by your luminosity, your love, your willingness to look inside my poems, and your ability to believe that not only is another existence possible, but we can fashion it from our own hands to open every door, disintegrate every ceiling, and do it all with a furious joy.

# Notes

The lynchings and events referenced in the collection are rooted in the history of the United States following the Treaty of Guadalupe Hidalgo. The ability to forget, reshape, and erase the histories of "the other" and the atrocities committed against "the other" by the United States, its agents and citizens, allow these acts to become part of the fabric of the nation. In this way, my appreciation to The Southern Poverty Law Center for documenting hate crimes and hate groups throughout the history of the nation, as well as to William D. Carrigan and Clive Web who wrote *Forgotten Dead; Mob Violence against Mexicans in the United States 1848-1928* (Oxford University Press, 2013), Nicholas Villanueva, Jr. who wrote *The Lynching of Mexicans in the Texas Borderlands* (University of New Mexico Press, 2017), and Ken Gonzalez-Day for his photography and conceptual art in *Erased Lynchings* and *Hang Trees*. Their art, documentation and scholarship was instrumental in helping stabilize the concept of this collection, and critical to ensure these histories remain accessible.

The photographs in "Standing here because my grandpa ran away from home to sell perfume en el Zócalo at 9" were sourced via Wikipedia Commons. "Caravana del hambre llegando al Zócalo de la Ciudad de México," which I edited to a black and white photo, is via Museo Archivo de la Fotografía, licensed under Creative Commons Attribution-Share Alike 3.0 Unported license (https://creativecommons.org/licenses/by-sa/3.0/deed.en). "Zocalo Ciudad de méxico 1940›s" is via Aurelio Escobar Castellanos and the Aurelio Escobar Castellanos Archive, licensed under Creative Commons Attribution 2.5 Generic License (https://creativecommons.org/licenses/by/2.5/deed.en).

The photograph in "In line I am a lot of things and since I am a lot of things I am everything he cannot imagine" was sourced via Heritage House Museum, [Hanging Tree - Orange, Texas], photograph, August 18, 1888; (https://texashistory.unt.edu/ark:/67531/metapth36665/: accessed April 21, 2018), University of North Texas Libraries, The Portal to Texas History, https://texashistory.unt.edu; via Heritage House Museum. It is without any known copyright restrictions.

The illustration in "A passport photo asks me to 2x2 myself and capture what I am in neutral and I recall I have yet to see the chamber of my heart turn tusk" is titled *Going After Ammunition* which appeared in W.E. Webb's *Buffalo Land* (E. Hannaford & Co., 1873). It is in the public domain with no known copyright restrictions.

The photograph in "Looks at me how Teddy Roosevelt died coveting a white buffalo" was taken by me while emptying my grandfather's work shed.

The images in "I am still, so still" were sourced from a series of photographs by Eadweard Muybridge titled *Animated sequence of a buffalo (American bison) galloping* first published in 1887 at Philadelphia (Animal Locomotion). It is in the public domain with no known copyright restrictions.

The source text for the erasure in "Prelude to a Mexican Lynching, February 2, 1848, Guadalupe Hidalgo; or The Treaty of Peace, Friendship, Limits, and Settlement" was from United States The Library of Congress, Statutes at Large, 1848, 922-942 (http://memory.loc.gov/cgi-bin/ampage?collId=llsl&fileName=009/llsl009.db&recNum=975) and features a parallel English and Spanish versions of the "Treaty of Peace, Friendship, Limits, and Settlement," aka "The Treaty of Guadalupe Hidalgo."

The image in "Framework" was sourced from The Miriam and Ira D. Wallach Division of Art, Prints and Photographs: Picture Collection, The New York Public Library. «Native women ; Native porter ; Lynch law in California.--Scene of the first execution in San Francisco, on June 10.» The New York Public Library Digital Collections. 1851-08-09. (http://digitalcollections.nypl.org/items/510d47e0-f821-a3d9-e040-e00a18064a99). It is without any known copyright restrictions.

"La Sirena, a Mexican Lynching, after the hanging death of Josefa Segovia in Downieville, CA July 5, 1851" is in a parallel conversation with the form of Vanessa Villarreal's poem "Malinche."

The image in "La Corona, a Mexican Lynching, No. 47" was sourced from Wikipedia Commons. The title of the illustrated poster is: "The head of the renowned bandit Joaquin Murrieta to be exhibited, as announced on this flyer, at the Stockton House on August 19, 1853. Ignacio Lisarraga of Sonora has given a sworn statement authenticating the identity of the head." It is in the public domain with no known copyright restrictions.

The poem "Artifacts on a Hanging Tree, Goliad, Texas (a series of 70 Mexican Lynchings, 1857" was initially drafted on June 23, 2018. I was conducting online research on trees associated with lynchings and hangings, and located the site for the Hanging Tree in Goliad, TX (https://www.tripadvisor.com/Attraction_Review-g55911-d7695172-Reviews-Hanging_Tree-Goliad_Texas.html). The location continues to receive positive reviews at the time of this printing.

The newspaper clippings in "Elegy of Skin, in Kerosene & Mesquite, Antonio Rodríguez, a Mexican Lynching, November 3, 1910" were sourced from *Sacramento Union*, Volume 120, Number 74, November 4, 1910.

The data cited in the footnotes of "La Maceta, a Mexican Lynching, in 7 artifacts, No. 52" is sourced via the following locations: "California Proposition 63: Language Attitudes Reflected in the Public Debate" by Susannah D.A. MacKaye (https://journals.sagepub.com/doi/10.1177/0002716290508001011) and from the State of California Secretary of State website "General Election - Statement of Vote, November 8, 1994" (https://www.sos.ca.gov/elections/prior-elections/statewide-election-results/general-election-november-8-1994/statement-vote/).

The clipped text that "A Request for Information: ICE - Regarding Immigration Detention Services Expansion, 2017 (Chicago, St. Paul, Detroit, Salt Lake City)" is in reference to a Request for Information Call issued by Immigration and Customs Enforcement (ICE) on October 12, 2017 to identify new detention sites near Chicago, IL., St. Paul, MN, Detroit, MI, or Salt Lake City, UT.

An italicized section of "Ojo" is in reference to a shooting in Rancho Tehama Reserve, CA on November 14, 2017. A *SFGate* quote from the murderer's friend is, "He had blue eyes, but I swear the color of his eyes changed recently. They went dark."

"The Desert is Circular, To Escape, Spiral" is a loosely translated quote from Alejandro Jodorowksy's film, *El Topo*.

"Cura for Exhaustion via Mirror" is in conversation with the photograph of James Ramirez titled "Borracho."

Anthony Cody is a CantoMundo fellow from Fresno, California. His poetry has appeared in *Gulf Coast*, *Ninth Letter*, *Prairie Schooner*, *TriQuarterly*, *The Boiler*, among other journals. Anthony is a member of the Hmong American Writers' Circle where he co-edited *How Do I Begin?: A Hmong American Literary Anthology*. As an MFA candidate at Fresno State, he serves as a fellow in the Laureate Lab Visual Wordist Studio started by Juan Felipe Herrera. In 2018, he received the Galway Kinnell Scholarship to attend the Community of Writers. He is the communications manager for CantoMundo, as well as an associate poetry editor for Noemi Press.

*Borderland Apocrypha*
Anthony Cody

Cover art by Josué Rojas
(Front cover: "Appropriate Strategies No. 2"
and back cover: "Appropriate Strategies No. 1")

Cover and interior set in Octavian MT Std and Perpetua Std

Cover and interior design by Gillian Olivia Blythe Hamel

Printed in the United States
by Books International, Dulles, Virginia
On 50# Glatfelter B19 Antique
Acid Free Archival Quality Recycled Paper

Publication of this book was made possible in part by gifts from
Katherine & John Gravendyk in honor of Hillary Gravendyk,
Francesca Bell, Mary Mackey, and The New Place Fund

Omnidawn Publishing
Oakland, California
Staff and Volunteers, Spring 2020

Rusty Morrison & Ken Keegan, senior editors & co-publishers
Kayla Ellenbecker, production editor
Gillian Olivia Blythe Hamel, senior editor & book designer
Trisha Peck, senior editor
Rob Hendricks, marketing assistant & *Omniverse* editor
Cassandra Smith, poetry editor & book designer
Sharon Zetter, poetry editor & book designer
Liza Flum, poetry editor
Matthew Bowie, poetry editor
Juliana Paslay, fiction editor
Gail Aronson, fiction editor
Izabella Santana, fiction editor & marketing assistant
SD Sumner, copyeditor